People and the Environment

by Jennifer Boothroyd

first step nonfiction

Lerner Publications Company · Minneapolis

People need
the **environment.**

People use the land
and its **resources.**

We use the land to
grow food.

We build homes on the land.

We use **oil** to make gas for
our cars.

We drink water.

People use animals
and plants.

We get food from animals.

Animals help us work.

We eat plants.

We make clothes
from **cotton.**

We burn wood for heat.

People **adapt** to their environment.

We wear warm clothes
when it gets cold.

We use boats to travel
on water.

People use the environment
in many ways.

People Hurt the Environment

We leave too much trash. Trash left on the ground and in the water hurts plants and animals.

We drive too many cars. Cars make air pollution.

We cut down
too many
trees in
one place.
Animals lose
their homes.

We spray too many chemicals
on plants. The chemicals are
washed into rivers and lakes.
These chemicals hurt the
plants and animals living there.

People Help the Environment

We recycle glass, metal, paper and plastic. These things can be made into something else.

We plant trees. Trees help clean the air and stop soil from washing away.

We ride
trains, buses,
and bikes, or
we walk.
Fewer cars
make less
air pollution.

We learn about
the environment.
People study
plants and
animals to know
how to help them.

Glossary

 adapt – change

 cotton – a plant that grows fibers around its seeds. The fibers are spun into thread.

 environment – the land, water, air, weather, and living things of the earth

 oil – a greasy liquid found underground; it is made into gasoline

 resources – things people use from nature

Index

The images in this book are used with the permission of: © Gavin Hellier/Robert Harding World Imagery/Getty Images, pp. 2, 22 (middle); PhotoDisc Royalty Free by Getty Images, pp. 3, 6, 18, 19, 20 (bottom), 21 (bottom), 22 (second from bottom, bottom); USDA, p. 4; © John R. Kreul/ Independent Picture Service, pp. 5, 7, 10; © Owen Franken/CORBIS, p. 8; © D. Hurst/Alamy, p. 9; © Royalty-Free/CORBIS, p. 11, 15; © Frank Seifert/The Image Bank/Getty Images, pp. 12, 22 (second from top); © Luc Beziat/Taxi/Getty Images, p. 13; © Dave Anthony/Taxi/Getty Images, pp. 14, 22 (top); © Frans Lemmens/Iconica/Getty Images, p. 16; © RubberBall Productions, p. 17; © Stockbyte, p. 20 (top); © Sam Lund/Independent Picture Service, p. 21 (top).

Front cover: © Mark Kelley/Stone/Getty Images

Lerner Publications Company
A division of Lerner Publishing Group, Inc.
241 First Avenue North
Minneapolis, MN 55401 U.S.A.

Website address: www.lernerbooks.com

Library of Congress Cataloging-in-Publication Data

Boothroyd, Jennifer, 1972-
        People and the environment / by Jennifer Boothroyd.
            p.   cm. — (First step nonfiction. Ecology)
        Includes index.
        ISBN 978-0-8225-8601-2 (lib. bdg. : alk. paper)
            1. Human ecology—Juvenile literature. 2. Human-plant relationships—
    Juvenile literature. 3. Human-animal relationships—Juvenile literature.
    I. Title.
    GF48.B66 2008
    304.2—dc22   2007007811

Manufactured in the United States of America
1 2 3 4 5 6 – DP – 13 12 11 10 09 08